Hidden in Plain Sight

In the shadows where whispers dwell,
Secrets echo, stories to tell.
A smile hides a world of pain,
Silent thoughts, like falling rain.

In crowded rooms, hearts can hide,
Veils of laughter worn with pride.
Behind the masks, a quiet fight,
Dancing shadows, lost in light.

Colors clash in the fading sun,
Each hue a dream, no longer fun.
Yet in the chaos, beauty thrives,
Hidden truths, where hope survives.

A fleeting glance across a room,
Soft glimmers spark in the gloom.
Where friendships bloom and rise anew,
Timeless tales in shades of blue.

In the mundane, the magic brews,
Every corner, a different view.
Life's tapestry, woven tight,
Ever present, out of sight.

Original title:
Beyond the Surface

Copyright © 2024 Swan Charm
All rights reserved.

Author: Swan Charm
ISBN HARDBACK: 978-9916-86-680-1
ISBN PAPERBACK: 978-9916-86-681-8
ISBN EBOOK: 978-9916-86-682-5

Reflections in Mysterious Waters

Beneath the veil of shimmering light,
Whispers dance, both soft and bright.
Mirrored thoughts in liquid hue,
Secrets held from me and you.

Ripples form with tales untold,
Glimpses of dreams in waters bold.
Floating leaves, a fleeting grace,
Nature's magic in this space.

Shadows cast by ancient trees,
Echoes carried on the breeze.
Each reflection sparks a sigh,
Invite the curious to try.

In silence deep, the waters stir,
Voices blend, a gentle slur.
Finding peace within the flow,
A tranquil mind, where thoughts can grow.

As dusk descends, the colors blend,
A symphony that has no end.
Reflections fade, yet leave a mark,
In mysterious waters, dreams embark.

The Depths of Silence

In the hush, where shadows creep,
Whispers hide, secrets keep.
Quiet moments stretch and yawn,
In the depth of stillness, dawn.

Voices lost beneath the waves,
Echoes linger in the caves.
Thoughts drift softly, pause and wait,
In silence, ponder the fate.

Empty spaces, filled with grace,
Silent wonders leave no trace.
Time stands still, a heavy sigh,
Lost in thoughts, we seldom fly.

Through the void, a heartbeat calls,
Faintly echoing through the halls.
In the depths, we find our way,
Silence speaks, come what may.

As light breaks in, we softly rise,
From the depths, a new surprise.
Each breath taken, a gentle start,
Find the silence in the heart.

Submerged Realities

Below the surface, lives entwined,
Hidden worlds, secrets aligned.
An ocean deep with dreams to share,
Submerged realities, everywhere.

Coral dances, colors blaze,
Underneath, a vivid maze.
Creatures glide through liquid dreams,
In the deep, nothing is as it seems.

Time drifts slowly, currents sway,
Moments lost, then slip away.
Ancient stories in the sand,
Whispers from a distant land.

Fathoms deep, the heart explores,
Unlocking each submerged door.
Truths unveiled by gentle tides,
In these depths, our soul confides.

As twilight falls, the waters gleam,
Mirrored visions, held like a dream.
In this depth, we find our grace,
Submerged realities, embrace.

Delving into the Unknown

A path untrodden, shadows play,
Curiosity leads the way.
Beneath the stars, the night unfolds,
Adventures wait, with tales untold.

Each twist and turn, the heart ignites,
Chasing wonders, chasing lights.
In the dark, we find our spark,
Delving deep into the dark.

Questions linger, answers hide,
In the mist, we must decide.
Carry dreams into the night,
Illuminate with inner light.

Through the fog, a vision glows,
What lies ahead, no one knows.
Fear dispels with every stride,
In the unknown, we abide.

As dawn approaches, shadows fade,
New horizons, unafraid.
Each journey broadens visions wide,
Delving deep, we find our pride.

The Depths of Daring

In shadows cast by doubt,
The heart beats strong and loud.
Step forth into the fray,
With courage as a shroud.

Each challenge, a new dawn,
A battle fought alone.
Yet in the depths we dive,
True bravery is grown.

Fear whispers in the dark,
But hope ignites the flame.
With every step we take,
The world will know our name.

We rise, we fall, we learn,
In trials, we find grace.
For in the depths of daring,
Our spirits learn to chase.

Embrace the winds of change,
For they will guide the brave.
In daring lies the magic,
A truth that we must crave.

Murmurs from the Dark Side

Silent whispers in the night,
Echoes of forgotten tales.
Shadowed corners hold their breath,
As mystery prevails.

Figures dance on the edge,
Where shadows seek to play.
The dark side calls to wander,
In its captivating sway.

Voices linger in the gloom,
Secrets wrapped in night.
Each murmur tells a story,
Of struggles out of sight.

Yet from the depths we rise,
With strength that feels like fire.
These whispers guide the way,
To our heart's true desire.

Embrace the dark and light,
For both can show the path.
In murmurs lie the answers,
To heartache and to wrath.

Peering Through the Veil

Behind the veil of silence,
Lies a world unknown.
Glimmers of connection,
In the shadows, they've grown.

Through the fog, we reach out,
For the warmth of a hand.
In whispered words of truth,
We learn to understand.

Each veil a thin divider,
Between moments lost and found.
Peering through its layers,
Is where our souls abound.

Curiosity ignites,
A flame that cannot stay.
For in the hidden depths,
Our truths will find their way.

Let's lift the veil together,
And wander hand in hand.
For through the haze of life,
We'll thrive where love withstands.

The Ocean of Untold Stories

Beneath the waves of time,
An ocean stretches wide.
Each story waits in stillness,
On the rolling tide.

Whispers of the ancients,
Sailors lost at sea.
Tales of joy and sorrow,
In waves that carry free.

Every shell a treasure,
Holding secrets deep.
The currents weave their magic,
In oceans vast and steep.

From shipwrecks to the stars,
The journeys never cease.
In this ocean of stories,
We find our inner peace.

So dive into the depths,
Where the heart learns to soar.
In the ocean of untold tales,
There's always room for more.

Beneath the Surface of Dreams

In whispers soft, the night unfolds,
Tales of silver, stories untold.
Beneath the stars, in silence we drift,
Searching deep for the heart's hidden gift.

Clouds of illusion, gently they sway,
Guiding our thoughts, leading astray.
With every breath, we delve further down,
Into the depths, away from the town.

Mirrored waters, a portal of light,
Cradling wishes in the heart of night.
Dancing reflections, shimmering dreams,
Pulling us close, unraveling seems.

Echoes of hope within shadows play,
Casting their glow along the way.
In the silence, we dare to believe,
That dreams are the path for our souls to weave.

Echoes of the Unvoiced

In the quiet, whispers take flight,
Voices stifled, seeking the light.
Each word unspoken, a story concealed,
In the shadows, their presence revealed.

Beneath the surface, emotions churn,
Learning the lessons we yearn to discern.
With every heartbeat, the echoes resound,
In the stillness, our souls are unbound.

A tapestry woven from silence and sound,
Threads of the lost, in whispers abound.
Finding connection in spaces unseen,
Linking our hearts through what might have been.

Reflections of thoughts held deep in our core,
Each unvoiced echo knocks softly at the door.
Letting it open, we step into grace,
Finding our truth in this sacred space.

Secrets of the Shadows

In the twilight, whispers begin,
Secrets hiding where the day grows thin.
Shadows linger, tales intertwine,
Guarding thoughts like a serpent's spine.

Nightfall drapes its cloak of black,
Veiling the past, never looking back.
In the corners, mysteries plead,
Yearning for souls to heed the unseen need.

Flickering candle, a guiding flame,
Illuminates fears, ignites the name.
With each flicker, a secret exposes,
The heart's journey where darkness composes.

Under the veil, truths softly sigh,
In shadows, we find the reasons to fly.
Embracing the unknown, we choose to explore,
The depths of the shadows that whisper for more.

The Unfolding Below

In the earth's cradle, life starts anew,
Roots intertwine, as morning breaks through.
Each layer reveals a story long lost,
In the soil's embrace, we treasure the cost.

Petals unfurl, like dreams in the dawn,
Tender and fragile, yet fiercely drawn.
Awakening whispers from beneath the ground,
The calling of life resonates profound.

Inhibition shed, we rise from the dark,
Awakening visions, igniting the spark.
The unfurling unfolds, a cycle divine,
In nature's rhythm, our spirits align.

With every heartbeat, the world sings along,
A symphony gentle, a resonant song.
In the unfolding, we discover our role,
Rooted in earth, yet reaching for soul.

Layers of Unwritten Tales

Beneath the ink, old stories hide,
Whispers swirl, like shadows they bide.
In pages unturned, dreams intertwine,
A symphony of life, both yours and mine.

Memories echo in silent night,
Words unsaid, concealed from sight.
Resilient hearts, with secrets to share,
Layer upon layer, stories laid bare.

Time, the weaver of fates unknown,
Crafts each moment, seeds we have sown.
In every heartbeat, a tale unfolds,
Boundless wonders, the future holds.

Through faded letters, the truth breaks free,
Chasing the echoes of what could be.
Each chapter a journey, every pause a breath,
In the layers of tales, we conquer death.

So write your story with courage and grace,
Unfurl the pages, let love's light embrace.
In the tapestry woven by dreams we create,
Layers of unwritten tales await.

The Dance of Invisible Currents

In the air, the whispers sway,
Invisible currents, where shadows play.
A twist, a turn, the world spins round,
In unseen realms, true magic is found.

The breeze carries secrets, soft and light,
With every moment, they ignite the night.
Hidden pathways where dreams take flight,
In shadows and silhouettes, hearts unite.

Beneath the surface, a rhythm beats,
Life's choreography in subtle feats.
Awake the senses, feel the embrace,
The dance of currents, a pas de deux grace.

With every heartbeat, the world expands,
Connected by threads, like unseen hands.
In the quiet lull, let your spirit soar,
As the dance of invisible currents implores.

So listen closely, the murmurs will tell,
Of the hidden currents, a mystic spell.
In life's gentle dance, let go, be free,
Dive deep into the flow of eternity.

The Mystique of the Depths

Beneath the surface, darkness hides,
A mystique unfolds where the silence abides.
Curling tendrils of secrets untold,
In the depths of the sea, mysteries unfold.

Echoes linger in the watery gloom,
Whispers of legends that softly bloom.
Time stands still in the ocean's embrace,
In the depths, the heart finds its place.

The dance of creatures, both strange and rare,
In shadows they flit, with delicate flair.
A world unseen, yet brimming with life,
In the calm of the depths, a soothing strife.

Glistening pearls rest on beds of sand,
Treasures concealed in a dreamer's hand.
With every dive, new wonders appear,
Each inch descended, shedding a tear.

So plunge into depths, where the heart yearns,
Embrace the mysteries; it's your turn to learn.
In the echoing silence, you're never alone,
In the mystique of the depths, the soul's truly known.

Through the Haze of Whispers

In the quiet fog, whispers roam,
A symphony of thoughts, far from home.
Unseen voices, where secrets entwine,
Through the haze, the heart will align.

Every breath carries stories untold,
Of dreams that flicker, both timid and bold.
In the twilight's veil, truth dances near,
As whispers emerge, wrapping us here.

Moments suspended, time stands still,
Murmurs of hope, an unspoken thrill.
In the depths of silence, find your voice,
Amidst the haze, let the heart rejoice.

Layers of echoes, soft as a sigh,
Through whispers and shadows, we'll learn to fly.
In the misty shroud, our spirits ignite,
Through the haze of whispers, embrace the light.

So follow the murmurs, let your heart lead,
In every soft whisper, plant the seed.
Through the haze, find the magic within,
In the dance of whispers, let your journey begin.

A Palette of Shadows

In twilight's grasp the colors blend,
Whispers of dusk where dreams descend.
Hues of mystery softly unfold,
A canvas of secrets, stories untold.

Shadows dance with silent grace,
Painting worlds in darkness' embrace.
Fingers trace the unseen path,
Finding solace in shadows' bath.

Each stroke lingers, a fleeting sigh,
Colors merging in the night sky.
A tapestry woven with fears and hope,
In this twilight, we learn to cope.

Fragments of light peek through the dark,
Illuminating every hidden spark.
A palette rich with shades of our plight,
In shadows we find our truest light.

Buried Wishes

In the earth where dreams lie deep,
Whispers of longing slowly creep.
Petals of hope in silence grow,
Tucked away where no one knows.

Fingers trace the sacred ground,
In each grain, a wish profound.
Time stands still as secrets breathe,
In the soil, our hopes bequeath.

Raindrops kiss the hidden seeds,
Nurturing them, fulfilling needs.
With the dawn, they yearn to rise,
Unfurling brightly 'neath open skies.

Yet buried deep they still remain,
Chained to whispers, dreams of pain.
But in the dark, they find their light,
Emerging bold to take their flight.

The Hidden Odyssey

In silent tides the journey flows,
Where every wave a tale bestows.
Maps of the heart, unwritten lore,
Leading us to the distant shore.

Stars above mark paths unknown,
Guiding souls who seek the throne.
With every step, a story spins,
Of battles lost and of newfound wins.

The wind carries secrets of time,
Echoes of courage in every climb.
Each corner turned, a lesson learned,
In the odyssey, the soul is burned.

Through jungled paths and mountains tall,
The heart stirs fiercely, answering the call.
With every heartbeat, we roam and roam,
Finding in wanderlust our true home.

Beneath the Glitter

In the sparkle where shadows dwell,
Lies a tale only time can tell.
Glistening shells on a tidal shore,
Hiding stories of old folklore.

Beneath the shimmer of gold-lit skies,
Lurks a truth that never dies.
Dreams adorned with sequins bright,
Masking sorrows in lavish light.

Yet under layers of gleaming grace,
Lies a world we often misplace.
Fragile hearts beneath the show,
Searching for warmth in the cold winds that blow.

With every glitter, a wish takes flight,
Dancing free through the velvet night.
But beneath the surface, we find our song,
In the echoes of where we belong.

Ripples of Lost Echoes

In the stillness of the night,
whispers float on the breeze,
memories dance like shadows,
yearning for forgotten dreams.

Each ripple tells a story,
sung by the moonlit sea,
soft echoes of the past,
calling out to you and me.

Waves crash with silent grace,
unfurling tales of old,
a symphony of lost voices,
wrapped in the sea's fold.

As dawn breaks the darkness,
colors bleed into the light,
we hold on to those echoes,
a fleeting, tender sight.

Though time may fade the whispers,
we carry them in our hearts,
in the ripples of the ocean,
a new journey never starts.

The Garden of Hidden Paths

In a garden rich with secrets,
where the sunlight barely plays,
a tapestry of emerald,
a maze of soft green ways.

Each turn holds a promise,
each bloom a whispered song,
a fragrance sweet and tender,
as nature's heart beats strong.

Beneath the ancient trellis,
a gentle breeze sighs low,
tales of wanderers untold,
where only few may go.

Footsteps veer from the main trail,
into shadows soft and deep,
in this garden of hidden paths,
we find our secrets keep.

Among the blooms in silence,
a world is born anew,
a symphony of wonders,
in every shade and hue.

Shattered Facades

Behind the painted smiles,
lies a story left untold,
aa visage cracked and weary,
a heart that's feeling cold.

Mirrors lie in broken shards,
each reflecting pain and fear,
a mask worn with precision,
holding back the silent tear.

Voices echo through the cracks,
a symphony of despair,
searching for an honest truth,
an openness so rare.

Yet within the shattered pieces,
a spark of hope remains,
a chance to rise from ashes,
and dance through all the rains.

For in the ruins of the past,
strength is found anew,
a beautiful resilience,
a spirit born to break through.

The Quiet Beneath the Roar

Amidst the thunderous silence,
where chaos leaps and soars,
a whisper hides in shadows,
beyond the raging wars.

The world may scream in fury,
with voices loud and stark,
yet in that wild tempest,
there's a quiet, glowing spark.

In moments filled with turmoil,
calm finds its hidden way,
like a lighthouse in the tempest,
guiding lost ships to stay.

Listen close, dear wanderer,
to the stillness within the storm,
a gentle, loving heartbeat,
a refuge safe and warm.

From the depths of roaring echoes,
a peace begins to rise,
in the quiet beneath the roar,
a truth that never dies.

Beneath the Mask of Tranquility

Calm waters hide the storm,
Whispers echo in the trees,
Beneath the smile, is a frown,
Truth is woven in the breeze.

Silent thoughts, a gentle guise,
A soft touch upon the heart,
Lies entwined in sweet disguise,
Peaceful art, a cautious start.

In the hush, a secret stirs,
Behind the eyes, a shadow plays,
Glimmers of light, and then—blurs,
Moments lost in quiet days.

Ripples dance on porcelain,
Yet inside, a tempest brews,
Fragile dreams, like glass, remain,
In serenity, the clues.

Unraveling the tangled threads,
Of what lies beneath the calm,
In the silence hunger spreads,
Seeking solace, seeking balm.

Secrets Lurking in Stillness

In the quiet, whispers dwell,
Faint and fleeting, soft and low,
Shadows weaving tales to tell,
Secrets bloom where few would go.

Every pause holds weight and time,
A heartbeat lost in golden air,
Stillness sings a quiet rhyme,
Murmurs drift without a care.

Beneath the surface, shadows hide,
Veiled in echoes of the past,
In silence, truths can be spied,
Frosty morning's breath, so vast.

A hushed promise, silent call,
In the depths of midnight's veil,
When all the world begins to fall,
Secrets lurk within the pale.

In the still, the heart can soar,
Silent stories found at dawn,
Finding more than what's in store,
Hidden truths, forever drawn.

The Intricacies of Hidden Depths

Depths below, a world unseen,
Layers sheltering what's true,
Beneath the masks we wear between,
Lies a tapestry of hue.

Twists and turns in every thought,
Butterflies in shadows play,
Hidden meanings, battles fought,
In the heart, they weave their stay.

A labyrinth of dreams and fears,
Echoes of forgotten hopes,
In silence, laughter meets our tears,
As we navigate the slopes.

The intricate patterns take their shape,
Following trails of light and dark,
Within each curve, a twist of tape,
Telling stories through the spark.

In the depths, we often find,
More than surface can reveal,
A dance of souls, each intertwined,
In secrets, our hearts conceal.

Navigating the Invisible

Patterns brush the unseen air,
Ghosts of thoughts that softly flow,
Mapping paths of hope and despair,
Where the hidden rivers glow.

In the void, we search for signs,
Echoes bouncing off the walls,
Through the mist, where fate entwines,
Cloaked in silence, time recalls.

Using instinct as our guide,
Through the haze, we weave our way,
Where the echoes choose to bide,
In the twilight break of day.

Though the lines of sight may blur,
Every heartbeat brings us near,
Navigating paths that stir,
As the unseen streams appear.

With each breath, the world unfolds,
Every pulse, a story shared,
In the invisible, life holds,
An embrace that's always bared.

The Depths of Illumination

In shadows deep, where whispers dwell,
A flicker glows, a sacred shell.
Each spark a guide, each beam a friend,
To hidden realms where dreams transcend.

Through tangled thoughts and veiled sights,
The heart ignites on endless nights.
With every glance, a truth reborn,
In light's embrace, the soul is worn.

Beneath the waves of doubt and fear,
A lighthouse shines to draw us near.
The depths awake, the surface yields,
To treasures locked in silent fields.

So seek the glimmer, chase the fire,
For in that glow, our souls aspire.
In every shadow, hope's refrain,
Illumination breaks the chain.

Layers of Mystique

Like veils of fog on ancient trees,
Each layer hides a silent breeze.
In solitude, the secrets dance,
While mystique lures with every glance.

Beneath the surface, stories lie,
In whispers soft, they yearn to fly.
A tapestry of dreams unfurls,
In hidden heartbeats, quiet swirls.

The moonlit paths that twist and turn,
Invite the soul to pause and learn.
Returning thoughts like tides that flow,
In depths of night, the wonders grow.

So peel the layers, seek the spark,
In shadows deep, igniting the dark.
For life's rich hues in silence speak,
In layers forged, the brave shall peek.

Currents of the Unexplored

Beneath the waves, a world awaits,
In currents wild, the heart creates.
With every tide, new tales emerge,
In depths unknown, our spirits surge.

Each ripple holds a quiet song,
That pulls us in, to where we belong.
The ocean vast, a boundless tome,
In every drop, we find our home.

So drift along this flowing stream,
Where unseen paths ignite our dream.
Adventure calls from distant shores,
In currents strong, life eversoars.

To sail the seas of the untried,
With open hearts and arms spread wide.
For in each wave, the courage grows,
In currents deep, our spirit knows.

The Horizon of Hidden Truths

At twilight's edge, the sky unfolds,
In hues of gold, the heart beholds.
With every glance, a doorway vast,
To truths concealed, to shadows cast.

The distant mountains beckon near,
In whispered winds, they draw our fear.
Yet with the dawn, a new belief,
In hidden paths, we find relief.

Beneath the surface, wonders rise,
In every gaze, a hidden prize.
So lift the veil, embrace the light,
For in the dark, the soul takes flight.

Chase down the dreams where shadows loom,
In quest for light, we find our bloom.
For at the edge, the truth awaits,
In horizons broad, love recreates.

Layers of Forgotten Dreams

Beneath the dust of time, they lay,
Whispers lost in yesterday's fray.
Each layer shells what once was bright,
Faded echoes in the night.

Once vibrant hues, now dulled and grey,
Memories flicker, then drift away.
In the silence, shadows creep,
Guarding secrets that we keep.

Fragments caught in tangled threads,
Tales of hope where sorrow spreads.
A canvas grand, but paint has dried,
Layered dreams that never sighed.

In twilight's grasp, I search for signs,
Lost ambitions, hidden lines.
Beneath the weight of all that's been,
Lies a spark, waiting to begin.

Time slips through like grains of sand,
Touch the past with gentle hand.
For in the layers, love remains,
A beacon bright through all the pains.

Secrets in the Shadows

In corners dark where whispers dwell,
Lies a tale no one will tell.
Secrets woven in the night,
Hidden truths just out of sight.

Shadows dance upon the wall,
Echoes of a silent call.
Veiled in mystery, cloaked in fear,
Fathomless, they linger near.

The moonlight casts its fleeting glow,
Revealing paths the heart won't know.
Every flicker, every sigh,
Draws the curtain, brings the lie.

Beneath the surface, currents churn,
In quiet hearts, the embers burn.
Secrets held, but not for long,
In the dark, we all belong.

So tread with care where shadows blend,
For every truth meets its end.
Unlock the doors that fear has sealed,
And find the light that's long concealed.

A World Unmasked

Underneath the painted smile,
Layers hide, a masquerade style.
Each facade a crafted art,
Concealing wounds within the heart.

We wear the masks to shield the pain,
Pretending joy where tears remain.
In crowded rooms, we stand alone,
Longing for a place called home.

The truth illustrates with bold strokes,
While whispered hopes become mere jokes.
Beneath the surface, thunder rolls,
A symphony of restless souls.

If we unveil what we conceal,
Perhaps the world can start to heal.
With every tear, a strength is found,
In vulnerability, we are bound.

So dare to step from shadows cast,
To let go of the weight of past.
A world unmasked, pure and bright,
Reveals the beauty in the light.

The Light Beneath the Veil

In softest mists, a glow resides,
A gentle warmth that never hides.
Beneath the veil, where shadows play,
The light awaits to find its way.

Through silken threads of doubt and fear,
Whispers of hope begin to clear.
With every breath, it sparks anew,
A guiding force in all we do.

Radiant dreams in the hidden space,
Illuminating each worn place.
The heart, a lantern, flickers bright,
Casting colors into night.

Hope shall rise, dispelling gloom,
A fragrant flower in full bloom.
For deep within, we hold the key,
To find the light that sets us free.

So let the veil fall to the ground,
Embrace the beauty that we've found.
In every heart, a flame resides,
Together, we are the guides.

Through the Lens of Obscurity

In twilight's grasp, whispers swell,
Secrets held where shadows dwell.
A world unseen, yet so near,
Cloaked in mist, wrapped in fear.

Glimmers fade, the edges blur,
Stories pulse in breathless stir.
Lost in thoughts, where memories play,
Time decays, slipping away.

Through veils thin, it's hard to see,
Paths entwined, yet bound to be.
Moments fade, like footprints on sand,
Leaving traces of life's grand plan.

A flicker sparks in restless night,
Guiding seekers toward the light.
Each step taken, a quiet dance,
Embrace the unknown, take a chance.

In obscurity, truths unfold,
Painting stories bold and old.
Embrace the dark and find your way,
Let the journey lead your stay.

Dances of Shadows and Light

In the twilight, shadows leap,
Whispers dance, secrets deep.
Light intertwines, soft and bright,
Creating forms in the fading night.

The rhythm flows, a silent song,
Moving swift, where we belong.
In every flicker, hearts ignite,
Tenebrous dreams take their flight.

Figures twirl, in the dark they glide,
Unity swells, no need to hide.
Through the chaos, we find our tune,
Bathed in beams of a silvery moon.

Melodies echo, a timeless art,
Binding souls, a world apart.
With every sway, shadows play,
Illuminated paths lead the way.

In this dance, we lose our fears,
Tracing patterns through the years.
Hand in hand, we'll take flight,
Together we shine, both dark and bright.

Unmasking the Quiet

In silence, secrets softly breathe,
Layers hidden, we dare to weave.
Beneath the calm, a tempest churns,
Yearning hearts, in silence, yearns.

Echoes hum, in realms unseen,
Voices beckon, sharp and keen.
In the hush, a story plays,
Waiting for the light of days.

Peel the mask, reveal the core,
Truths emerge, they can't ignore.
In the quiet, courage grows,
Whispers bloom, like fragile rose.

Step by step, unveil the sight,
Shadows shift, embrace the light.
Every heartbeat speaks in grace,
Unmasking fears, finding our place.

With tender hands, we gently pry,
Opening hearts, letting them fly.
In the quiet, we're no longer shy,
Together we soar, to the endless sky.

Beneath the Glittering Surface

Beneath the gleam, lies the unknown,
A world of whispers, all our own.
Hidden depths, where dreams collide,
Beneath the surface, truths abide.

Rippling waves, reflecting light,
Fates entwined, caught in the night.
Every shimmer hides a tale,
In the depths, we will prevail.

Journey forth, into the deep,
Where secrets linger, shadows creep.
In the abyss, sparkles gleam,
Awakening our boldest dream.

As we dive through layers thick,
A glint of hope, we often pick.
Beneath the glamour, what's concealed,
A treasure trove, yet unrevealed.

Collect the pearls, embrace the dive,
From hidden worlds, we come alive.
In the dance of depths and heights,
We find our truth, our heart ignites.

Threads of Distant Echoes

In the quiet of the night,
Whispers dance like ghosts,
Memories entwined in light,
Carried by the utmost.

Voices linger in the air,
Tales from ages past,
Fleeting moments, soft and rare,
In shadows they are cast.

Each thread a story spun,
Woven through the ages,
Life and loss, the battles won,
Written on the pages.

Time unveils its mystic art,
In echoes found anew,
Every feeling, every heart,
In threads that still hold true.

We'll tread where echoes lead,
In dreams that never cease,
For in each heart, a seed,
Of whispered, timeless peace.

Beneath the Forgotten

Beneath the veil of dust,
Lies a world untold,
Secrets hidden, lost in rust,
In shadows, silent gold.

Ruins whisper soft and low,
Of lives once lived with fire,
Ghostly echoes ebb and flow,
Among the lost desire.

Each stone a tale so deep,
Of laughter, pain, and tears,
In memories that we keep,
For countless, silent years.

Nature reclaims her throne,
With roots and vines that creep,
In places once well-known,
Where silence holds its sweep.

Yet hope flickers like a flame,
In shadows carved by time,
For every place has name,
In heartbeats, an unseen rhyme.

The Untold Journey

A path stretched out before me,
Each step a whispered choice,
In shadows, truths to see,
In silence, hear the voice.

Footprints marked by dreams I seek,
In valleys low and high,
Every turning, every peak,
Beneath the open sky.

The winds of change will blow,
With stories left unspun,
In every new tomorrow,
Life's tapestry undone.

Stars will guide my wandering,
Through night's embrace so vast,
In every heart, a wondering,
Of futures tied to past.

And as horizons beckon bright,
With treasures yet to find,
The journey holds its light,
In every soul entwined.

The Realm Beneath the Waves

Beneath the surface, secrets lie,
In depths of azure seas,
Whispers of the waves that sigh,
A lost world's memories.

Coral kingdoms rise and fall,
In colors bright and bold,
Echoes of a siren's call,
In stories yet untold.

Anemones dance with grace,
In tidal rhythms sweet,
Where creatures roam, a hidden space,
In currents, life's heartbeat.

Above, the world can seem so grand,
Yet treasures often hide,
In silence, as the ocean's hand,
Cradles them with pride.

So let us dive into the blue,
To realms we've yet to see,
For in the depths, life starts anew,
Where dreams and waters free.

Skeletons in the Silent Sea

Beneath the waves, the shadows sleep,
Ancient whispers, secrets keep.
Faded bones, stories told,
Lost in depths, too dark and cold.

Echoes linger, haunting sighs,
Ghostly figures beneath the ties.
Silent towns of coral gray,
Skeletons in the silent bay.

Sunlight struggles, not a trace,
Of the lives that once found grace.
Buried tales, like pearls in sand,
Lost to time, a forgotten land.

Every tide brings back the night,
Visions dance in fleeting light.
With every wave, a story wakes,
In the sea, the stillness quakes.

A treasure lies where none can see,
In the heart of the silent sea.
Echoing dreams, they drift away,
Skeletons in the sea's ballet.

Delving into Forgotten Echoes

In the echoes of what once was,
Whispers linger without a pause.
Faded footsteps on dusty stone,
Delving deep, we are not alone.

Forgotten halls, dimly lit,
Every corner has tales to fit.
Voices rise with trembling grace,
Cascading notes from a lost place.

Time stands still, yet flies away,
Chasing shadows at end of day.
Memories wrapped in dust and time,
Reverberations, soft as rhyme.

Heartbeats echo through the years,
Moments captured, laughed and teared.
With each breath, the past awakes,
Delving deep, the silence breaks.

History's thread is thin and gold,
Stories waiting to be told.
Echoes linger, soft yet clear,
Forgotten whispers drawing near.

Reflections Underneath the Calm

Mirror of the still blue tide,
Secrets in the depths abide.
Floating dreams on the water's skin,
Reflections where the light wears thin.

Underneath the glassy sheen,
Lie the truths that sit unseen.
Waves may ripple but don't divide,
What is hidden, deep inside.

Thoughts submerged like ships of yore,
Drifting softly to the shore.
In the calm, the mind can roam,
Finding fragments of a home.

Breaking through the tranquil glass,
Every moment cannot pass.
Glimmers of a distant thought,
Reflections of the battles fought.

Embrace the stillness of the night,
Trust the depths, embrace the light.
In the quiet, we may find,
Reflections of a hopeful mind.

The Depth of Lost Dreams

In the chasm where dreams descend,
Silent whispers start to blend.
Shattered hopes drift like the mist,
In the depths of the heart's twist.

Each lost dream tells a tale of old,
A memory wrapped in silver and gold.
Flickers of light, they soon unfold,
In the quiet, stories bold.

Depths that tremble with each sigh,
Vows once spoken, now ask why.
Chasing shadows, we learn to bend,
A journey that can never end.

Underneath the weight of time,
Lost ambitions quietly chime.
Through the dark, we seek the spark,
As embers fade, we light the dark.

Tides will wash away the fear,
In the silence, dreams draw near.
The depth of lost dreams does not die,
Each heartbeat brings a chance to fly.

Treasures of the Abyss

In the silence of the deep,
Golden dreams lie still and sleep.
Glistening pearls, a hidden lore,
Secrets whispered from the shore.

Creatures dance in ghostly light,
Silent shadows in the night.
Caverns hold their ancient tales,
Echoes drift through subaqueous trails.

A sunken ship, a faded mast,
History trapped in shadows cast.
Rusty coins and broken dreams,
Lost in time, or so it seems.

Glimmers flash in darkened caves,
Guarded well by ocean waves.
Each treasure tells a story rare,
Of love and loss, of hope laid bare.

Dive into the unknown sea,
Where past and present drift freely.
In the abyss, life still flows,
A world of wonders, ever glows.

The Silent Symphony

In shadows cast by evening's glow,
A melody begins to flow.
No notes are played, no voices sing,
Yet silence speaks of everything.

Leaves rustle gently in the breeze,
Nature's rhythm, a soft tease.
Crickets chirp, a quiet song,
In this space, where dreams belong.

Stars twinkle in the velvet night,
A symphony of purest light.
Each blink a note, each shimmer, sound,
In darkness, harmony is found.

The moon, a maestro, guides the tones,
Through whispered winds, and ancient drones.
In silence, we can truly hear,
The songs of life that draw us near.

Close your eyes and drift away,
Let the silence softly sway.
In this realm of quiet bliss,
Find the symphony, the hidden kiss.

Veiled Emotions

Behind the mask, a heart concealed,
Deep within, the truth revealed.
Joy and sorrow, side by side,
In shadows where the secrets hide.

Laughter echoes, a fleeting sound,
Yet within, a weight profound.
Eyes can sparkle, smiles can gleam,
But veils can guard the deepest dream.

Words unsaid hang in the air,
Silent wishes, a weight to bear.
Yearning glances, unspoken fears,
In the quiet, the heart appears.

Hope entwined with threads of pain,
A tapestry of joy and rain.
Each layer hides a sacred tale,
In veiled emotions, we set sail.

Bravely we wear our veils of grace,
Seeking truth in every face.
Through the layers, we will find,
The beauty woven in mankind.

Whispers of the Depths

In the stillness of the night,
Softly comes a distant light.
Whispers float on gentle tide,
Secrets that the shadows hide.

In the depths where silence dwells,
Echoes weave enchanted spells.
Every ripple, a story spun,
Of battles lost and victories won.

The ocean's heart, a timeless place,
Holding dreams in its embrace.
Casting nets of hope and fear,
In its depths, we draw near.

Voices linger, faint and low,
Carried by the currents flow.
Each whisper brings a truth to light,
Guiding souls through darkened plight.

Listen close, the depths will speak,
Beyond the surface, the strong and weak.
In every whisper, a thread of fate,
In the abyss, we contemplate.

Lurking in Stillness

In shadows thick, the silence dwells,
Where whispers weave their haunting spells.
A calm disguise, yet secrets flow,
Beneath the still, the currents glow.

In corners dark, the silence stings,
A waiting hush, the tension clings.
With bated breath, the world stands still,
As time unfolds, a ghostly thrill.

Beneath the surface, movements fade,
A dance of dreams, a masquerade.
In every pause, a story speaks,
In stillness deep, the soul seeks peaks.

The echoes linger, softly tread,
In quiet realms, the shadows spread.
A lullaby of thoughts concealed,
In stillness, hearts are often healed.

In hidden depths, the lurkers wait,
For moments bold to captivate.
In silence thick, the truth lays bare,
As stillness reigns, we learn to care.

A Journey into the Deep

Beneath the waves, the wonders lie,
In depths unseen, where fish learn to fly.
A silent dive, into the blue,
Where mysteries wait, for me and you.

Each stroke a whisper, buoyant dreams,
In ocean's heart, the sunlight beams.
The currents twist, and secrets rise,
In liquid realms, where magic flies.

Time flows like tides, in ebb and flow,
Exploring depths, where few dare go.
A vivid world of colors bright,
In watery realms, each turn's a flight.

The creatures dance, in balletic grace,
In every wave, a new embrace.
From coral caves to sandy beds,
A journey deep, where few have tread.

With every heartbeat, a story swells,
Of ancient dreams and ocean's spells.
A voyage vast, through depths we glide,
Into the blue, with hearts open wide.

Fathoms of Hidden Truth

Beneath the layers, the truth lies low,
In shadows thick, where few dare go.
Each fathom deep, a tale untold,
Whispers of lives, both brave and bold.

In murky waters, secrets stir,
In silence vast, the echoes purr.
A quest for light, a search for grace,
Through tangled dreams, we find our place.

Like ships adrift, our thoughts collide,
In hidden realms, where hopes abide.
With every dive, the depths reveal,
The weight of truth, a heart to feel.

In waters dark, reflections gleam,
Of things once lost, the fading beam.
With every splash, the moments flow,
Into the depths, where few will go.

In fathoms deep, we find our way,
Through hidden truths, we learn to sway.
The journey long, yet worth the strife,
In depths unknown, we find our life.

Enigma of the Unseen

In mystic realms, the shadows play,
An enigma waits, in hues of gray.
Where whispers flee, and visions blend,
The unseen paths, lead without end.

Through veils of time, the echoes blend,
A tender call, a longing send.
In secret places, truth expands,
In twilight's grasp, a world commands.

The heartbeats pulse, in hidden sync,
In mirrored pools, where thoughts can think.
A riddle dances, in moonlight's glow,
An unseen hand, where few can go.

As shadows shift, the truth takes flight,
In every flicker, there's hidden light.
A journey spun, through time and space,
The unseen guide, our constant grace.

Though mysteries cloak, we'll find the way,
In enigma's arms, we'll learn to sway.
For in the dark, where secrets hide,
The unseen spark, ignites our stride.

Discoveries Beneath the Ice

Beneath the frost, a secret waits,
Ancient whispers through icy gates.
Crystal structures, tales unwind,
Nature's craft, both cruel and kind.

Time stands still in frozen air,
Echoes linger, stark and bare.
Each shard tells of years gone by,
A history written in the sky.

Lakes of blue in a solid sea,
Mirrored dreams of what must be.
Bubbles trapped, a frozen breath,
Life once lived, now dances with death.

Colors shimmer, visions bright,
Hidden worlds, lost to sight.
In silence deep, truths reside,
Waiting for the frozen tide.

What once was lost will soon be found,
Where icy depths hold wisdom profound.
In every layer, stories persist,
Discoveries waiting in the twist.

Veins of the Earth

Rivers coursing through the land,
Veins that pulse, both strong and grand.
Beneath the soil, life resides,
In quiet places, nature hides.

Roots entwine in silent grace,
Finding shelter, holding space.
Each fracture tells of time's embrace,
Life's essence woven, interlaced.

Mountains rise, a steadfast wall,
Echoes of ancient giants call.
Through stone and dust, a story flows,
In every crevice, life bestows.

Minerals sleep in darkened caves,
Guardians of secrets, wise and brave.
Nature's art, a canvas vast,
Whispers of ages, shadows cast.

The heartbeat strong beneath our feet,
In every pulse, a truth complete.
Feel the rhythm, know her worth,
In the veins that bind the Earth.

Under the Dull Surface

Beneath the calm, a storm may brew,
Ripples hide what's false and true.
A gentle mask, and yet it lies,
What's under wraps may mesmerize.

Shadows shift in murky depths,
Secrets tangled in silent steps.
Every sigh beneath the wave,
A world so close, yet none can save.

The weight of silence, thick and low,
Hides the tales that wish to flow.
In the hush, a heartbeat waits,
A whisper paused at nature's gates.

Life finds ways, despite the gray,
Colors hidden, yearning for day.
What lies beyond the surface dull,
Is life unspoken, beautiful.

Dive a little, break the skin,
Unlock the wonders held within.
Under the dull, there lies a spark,
A lively world that's rich and dark.

Ocean of Untold Stories

Waves crash down with a mighty roar,
Each one carries tales of yore.
Deep below, the currents weave,
An ocean's heart, in hope we believe.

A sailor's dream, a tempest's rage,
The sea's vast tome, a turning page.
Each whispered tale, both lost and found,
In depths where secrets swirl around.

Coral kingdoms, bright and bold,
Guardians of stories yet untold.
Creatures roam in endless quest,
In watery realms, they'll find their rest.

Old wrecks rest where silence reigns,
Shells hold whispers of ships and chains.
What treasures lie in depths of blue,
Waiting for eyes to see them true?

With every tide, the past draws near,
A voice of history, pure and clear.
In this ocean, vast and free,
Unfold the mysteries of the sea.

Unveiling the Depths

In silent waters, secrets hide,
Waves whisper tales, where dreams abide.
Life's reflections dance and sway,
Drawing hearts to the ocean's play.

Beneath the surface, mysteries bloom,
Softly they call, dispelling the gloom.
Every ripple tells a story true,
In the depths, a world anew.

Currents rise, with stories old,
In shades of azure, treasures unfold.
Hope gathers like sea foam's crest,
In each wave, life finds its rest.

Glimmers of light break through the blue,
A journey begins, for me and you.
To seek the wonders, to dare the deep,
In the ocean's heart, our souls we'll keep.

So dive, dear friend, the depths await,
Embrace the tides, don't hesitate.
With open hearts, let the voyage start,
Unveiling the depths, a work of art.

Beneath the Whispering Leaves

In dappled light, the branches sway,
Whispers of nature shape the day.
Secrets rustle in the breeze,
Inviting thoughts among the trees.

Each leaf a story, ancient and wise,
Echoing softly beneath the skies.
Roots entwined in earth so deep,
Guarding the dreams that we dare to keep.

As twilight drapes its gentle veil,
Shadows lengthen, softening the trail.
Moonlight filters through the green,
Casting wonders, serene, unseen.

Creatures stir in the silken night,
A symphony of dreams takes flight.
Beneath the whispering leaves we find,
A refuge for the wandering mind.

So let the forest cradle your heart,
In every sound, you'll find a part.
Beneath the leaves, in stillness, breathe,
Discover the magic nature weaves.

The Clarity of Shadows

In the twilight, shadows play,
Mysterious forms that drift away.
The dance of light and dark entwined,
In the silence, answers find.

Glimmers of truth in the obscured,
Whispers of hopes that feel assured.
A canvas painted, dusk and dawn,
In shadows' depth, our fears are gone.

With every shade, a story told,
In quiet moments, we grow bold.
Through murky paths, we venture forth,
In the dark, we glimpse our worth.

Echoes linger in the cool night air,
Soft reminders of dreams laid bare.
The clarity found in the subtle game,
With shadows around, we're not the same.

So embrace the night, let worries cease,
In the shadows, there's profound peace.
For in every shadow, a light shall gleam,
In the dance of darkness, let us dream.

Discoveries of the Deep

Beneath the waves, worlds unite,
Colorful wonders, pure delight.
Coral forests, currents flow,
In this realm, our spirits grow.

Whale songs echo through the dark,
In the depths, we leave a mark.
Mysteries hidden, treasures found,
In ocean's cradle, we are bound.

Jellyfish drift, like dreams in space,
A ballet of life in endless grace.
Tales written in the sand and foam,
In the sea's embrace, we find our home.

Stars above reflect the sea,
In watery realms, we are set free.
Exploring depths, we seek and learn,
In the heart of the ocean, passions burn.

So dive with wonder, let your heart leap,
In the vastness of blue, secrets keep.
Discover the joys that the deep would share,
In every wave, a promise rare.

Whispers Beneath the Waves

Whispers dance in salty air,
Secrets of the ocean's lair.
Dreams are woven, soft and light,
Beneath the waves, in deep of night.

Fishes glimmer, shadows glide,
Currents pull as tides confide.
Mysteries wrap like velvet cloth,
Nature's voice, a solemn oath.

Coral thrones in colors bright,
Guardians of the hidden light.
Songs of silence, echoes fade,
In the depths where dreams are laid.

Underneath, a world concealed,
Secrets spent, yet never revealed.
Drifting softly, spirits call,
In the deep, we hear it all.

Bubbles rise with tales untold,
Wonders of the deep unfold.
Every ripple, every sway,
Whispers call from far away.

Hidden Depths

In hidden depths, the shadows play,
Where sunlight fails to find its way.
Echoes linger in the gloom,
Whispers hint of life to bloom.

Beneath the rocks, the secrets sleep,
In swirling tides, the mysteries keep.
Veils of water, layered thick,
Intangible, a clock that ticks.

Creatures shy, with colors rare,
Move with grace, beyond despair.
In this world of dark and light,
Hidden depths ignite the night.

Every swell tells a tale profound,
In the silence, wisdom's found.
Deeper still, the heartbeats flow,
Muffled songs from below.

A realm where time dissolves away,
In hidden depths, we long to stay.
Waves may rise and crash above,
Yet here, we find a different love.

The Unseen Horizon

Beyond the waves, where skies merge blue,
The unseen horizon calls to you.
Promises dance like distant stars,
Hiding truths in cosmic bars.

Where dreams collide with ocean's mist,
Time and space twist and twist.
In the twilight, visions gleam,
Gathering lost, forgotten dreams.

Each horizon holds a story tight,
Of sailors lost in endless night.
In the deep where few have trod,
Consigned to silence, soundless nod.

Yet hope emerges from the deep,
To wake the dreams that still may sleep.
Through unseen paths, we bravely roam,
In hearts of wanderers, find our home.

Beyond the waves, the journey calls,
Forward still, despite the falls.
In the distance, horizons fade,
But the adventure never strayed.

Echoes from the Abyss

Echoes rise from depths unknown,
Whispers of the sea's soft moan.
Voices drift in shadows deep,
Guarding secrets that they keep.

In the abyss, where silence reigns,
Life's symphony, in gentle strains.
Currents weave a tapestry,
Of ancient tales that set us free.

From sunken ships to coral graves,
Echoes tell of daring saves.
Ghosts of mariners, brave and bold,
Sharing dreams in waters cold.

The tide pulls back, a deep embrace,
Rising spirits find their place.
Lost within the ocean's heart,
In the abyss, we are all part.

As echoes fade, new stories rise,
In every wave, a world that sighs.
In the dark, we learn to glean,
Whispers from the unseen scene.

Tracing Ripples of the Unknown

In silence, waters stretch and sway,
Echoes whisper secrets, they gently play.
Each ripple dances, a fleeting sign,
Leads to the hidden, a world divine.

Beneath the surface, shadows weave,
Mysteries linger, we dare to believe.
Curiosity whispers, a siren's call,
Inviting adventurers to risk it all.

A journey begins with a single thought,
In the depths of longing, an answer sought.
We delve into realms where few have tread,
Tracing the ripples, where hopes are fed.

With each step forward, the unknown grows near,
The heart beats faster, amidst joy and fear.
One bold leap can change the fate,
To uncover wonders, oh, how they await!

Boundless horizons, where dreams unfurl,
In the dance of water, we find our pearl.
The journey of seeking, the thrill it brings,
Tracing the ripples, we find our wings.

Gazing into the Hidden Depths

Open your eyes to the world below,
A realm of secrets, its wonders glow.
In silence, we peer with yearning souls,
Into the depths where the heart unfolds.

The shadows whisper, stories untold,
In glimmers of light, mysteries unfold.
Each glance reveals what lies in wait,
Gazing into layers that time creates.

In the stillness, we lose and we find,
The echoes of longings entwined in the mind.
The depths are vast, with treasures to seek,
Gazing deeper, the future can speak.

As waters churn, they mirror the skies,
Reflections of dreams and fated ties.
Through veils of doubt, we start to see,
Gazing into depths, we learn to be free.

To touch the essence, to feel the embrace,
Of moments forgotten, a sacred place.
We dive into knowing, no longer lost,
Gazing into depths, we rise from the frost.

With each gentle wave, the soul finds its way,
In the deepening dark, we welcome the day.
Through eyes wide open, the quiet surges,
Gazing into depths, the heart emerges.

The Underbelly of Daylight

When morning breaks, the shadows sink,
Beneath the light, a world to think.
Where colors clash and shapes distort,
The underbelly hides its retort.

Sunshine dances, yet darkness clings,
In the corners where silence rings.
The vibrant hues mask the cries,
Of hidden truths beneath the lies.

A tapestry woven with threads of fate,
Where hope and sorrow oft hesitate.
Each day reveals a different face,
In the underbelly, the heart finds grace.

As shadows flicker, they speak in tongues,
Stories of old, where the past still clung.
Through brightened halls and grayed-out ways,
The underbelly tells of lost days.

Embrace the struggle and honor the fight,
For in the dark, we find our light.
Journey with courage, embrace the fear,
The underbelly whispers, "You're near."

In twilight's glow, we learn to see,
The dance of contrasts, both you and me.
The sunlight fades, yet truths ignite,
In the underbelly of daylight.

Unearthing the Unseen

Beneath the soil, where roots entangle,
Life pulses quietly, mysteries dangle.
Each gentle sigh can stir the ground,
Unearthing truths that still abound.

In whispers of winds that sweep the plains,
Echoes of history, love, and pains.
Buried deep, the stories long gone,
Unearthing the unseen, we discover dawn.

As fingers sift through the earthly shards,
Fleeting moments become our guards.
In every touch, a memory gleams,
Unearthing the unseen reveals our dreams.

To wander through fields of ancient lore,
The heart beats louder, craving more.
In the stillness, the past converses,
Unearthing the unseen, our soul immerses.

As roots intertwine, they guide our way,
Lessons from ages come out to play.
In nature's arms, we're not alone,
Unearthing the unseen, we find our home.

With patience and love, we learn to grow,
In fields of wonder where few dare go.
Unearthing treasures with each small stride,
To dance with the unseen, our hearts open wide.

Masked Realities

In shadows deep, secrets creep,
Faces hide what hearts keep.
Behind the veil, truth disguised,
In silence, the soul cries.

Whispers lost, tales untold,
Courage wanes, fears unfold.
Each mask worn, a story's thread,
In every glance, a dream dead.

Life's theater, roles we play,
In the spotlight, we sway.
Chasing light, we fear the fall,
Yet we dance, to heed the call.

Fragments break, reflections fade,
In the maze, our choices laid.
Hidden truths in the masquerade,
In the shadows, courage prayed.

At the end, what will reveal,
The depth of wounds that never heal?
Masked realities intertwine,
In the heart, where secrets shine.

The Other Side of Reflection

In mirrors' depths, a world awaits,
Each glance unveils a truth of fates.
Beyond the glass, a place unknown,
Where whispers dwell and thoughts have grown.

Shadows dance with fleeting grace,
Chasing dreams we long to face.
What lies beyond that glimmer bright,
A vision lost in endless night?

Echoes call from realms unseen,
Through the fog, we seek the green.
A journey starts with heart in hand,
To step beyond and learn to stand.

Reflections speak in muted tones,
The stories old, the silent groans.
In layers thick, our fears conceal,
Yet through the veil, we learn to heal.

On the other side, we rise,
With open hearts, embracing skies.
In every shard, a promise lies,
To find the truth that never dies.

Hidden Pathways

A winding road, where secrets flow,
In tangled woods, the wild winds blow.
Where every step leads us anew,
To places hidden from our view.

Beneath the leaves, the whispers dwell,
In every corner, tales to tell.
With every twist, and every turn,
The heart ignites, the spirit yearns.

Footsteps stray on ancient ground,
Lost in thought, where truths abound.
The signs are faint, yet guide the way,
Through shadows deep, into the day.

Amidst the thorns, blooms the rarest flower,
Where hope is found in darkest hour.
Each hidden path a choice to make,
In every heartbeat, life's awake.

So journey forth, with courage bright,
Through tangled woods into the light.
For every pathway we explore,
A piece of us forever stored.

The Complex Tides

Waves crash hard against the shore,
In rhythmic dance, they rise and pour.
The ocean's voice, a mournful sigh,
Where dreams are lost and hopes float by.

Beneath the surface, secrets churn,
In depths profound, we yearn and learn.
Currents pull, then gently tease,
In changing winds, the heart finds ease.

The moon commands the night's embrace,
With every phase, we find our place.
As tides return, we rise to meet,
The ebb and flow, a bittersweet.

Beneath the storm, calm waters lie,
In chaos reigns, the spirit flies.
To navigate the wild unknown,
In every rise, we find our home.

So dance with waves, let worries glide,
Embrace the pull of complex tides.
For through the storm, we learn to sail,
In every breath, there's a new tale.

Whispers Beneath the Waves

Beneath the foam, a secret lies,
Where whispers dance in soft goodbyes.
The ocean breathes, a silent hymn,
As twilight dims, and lights grow dim.

Waves caress the sandy shore,
A lullaby from ocean's core.
With every tide, the story's told,
Of ancient love and treasures bold.

Shells whisper tales of ships long gone,
In twilight's glow, they weave and spawn.
Secrets deep with each swell and fall,
An ageless echo, a siren's call.

The moonlight casts a silver glow,
On water's face, a softening flow.
Night shadows play where dreams take flight,
Whispers of realms hidden from sight.

In depths unknown, the heart remains,
In currents swift, love's gentle chains.
Forever bound in salty embrace,
Where whispers linger, time cannot trace.

Echoes of the Abyss

In darkened depths where shadows creep,
Echoes linger, secrets keep.
A caverned heart, a hidden space,
Where time and light lose their grace.

Glimmers tease, then fade away,
As whispers stir the silent bay.
Lost sailors sing their somber tunes,
While silence swells beneath the moons.

The pressures rise, the stillness thicks,
In watery halls, the heart convicts.
Murk and tide conceal their breath,
An all-consuming, silent death.

Mysteries swirl like currents strong,
In darkened chambers where they belong.
Fragments of voices, both near and far,
Call from depths, like a fleeting star.

With every pulse, the abyss sighs,
As ancient whispers intertwine with ties.
The language of the deep resounds,
In echoes lost, where silence drowns.

Secrets Hidden in Depths

Beneath the waves, where darkness sighs,
Lie secrets bound by water's ties.
The depths conceal a world unseen,
Where shadows stretch, and dreams convene.

Sunken ships with tales untold,
Guarded by the ocean's hold.
A treasure map of hearts once brave,
Now rests in peace beneath the wave.

Currents carve their stories deep,
Where ancient giants twist and sweep.
Silences speak in tongues of old,
As waves embrace the tales of gold.

Anemones sway in gentle grace,
Hiding wonders that time can't erase.
Every ripple carries a breath,
Of tales that dance with life and death.

In hidden grottos, silence reigns,
Yet whispers pulse in soft refrains.
The depths are rich with vibrant hues,
Where secrets bloom, and time renews.

Veils of Unseen Realms

Beyond the surface, veils entwined,
A dance of realms, by light defined.
Shadows play where visions blend,
In water's womb, all things transcend.

A shimmering mist around me swirls,
Breath of dreams in liquid curls.
Unseen realms with whispered breath,
Where echoes linger, life and death.

Fathoms deep, where light refracts,
Beauty dwells in soft impacts.
Secrets curl like waves in flight,
In the silence of the twilight.

Bubbles rise from worlds below,
Carrying tales of ebb and flow.
With each burst, a truth is freed,
In currents fierce, in silence's creed.

Veils of wonder shimmer bright,
In depths that cradle day and night.
A tapestry of dreams unfolds,
Where unseen realms are strong and bold.

Beneath the Shimmering Veil

Beneath the shimmering veil, the night sings,
Whispers of dreams and forgotten things.
Stars twinkle in a dance of light,
Guiding the heart through the silent night.

The moon hangs low, a silver coin,
Casting shadows where secrets join.
Gentle breezes weave through trees,
Carrying tales on the midnight breeze.

In the quiet, hope takes flight,
Embracing shadows with soft delight.
Each twinkle above holds a wish,
A spark of magic in the night's dish.

Together we wander, hand in hand,
Lost in the wonder, wherever we stand.
Beneath the shimmer, dreams are made,
A touch of the night, memories laid.

So hush your fears, let silence prevail,
Embrace the night, beneath the veil.
For every moment wrapped in starlight,
Holds the promise of a new dawn's light.

The Core of Hidden Currents

In the depths where secrets swirl,
Hidden currents dance and twirl.
Beneath the surface, whispers flow,
Tales of the heart, few will know.

Rippling waters, soft and still,
Echoes of desires, dreams to fulfill.
Every wave a fleeting spark,
Carving paths in the quiet dark.

Time holds its breath, the world slows down,
As mysteries rise, crown to crown.
In the heart of silence, wisdom lies,
Waiting to surface, beneath the skies.

The eddies draw us closer near,
To the core where we lose our fear.
In each current, a story's spun,
Revealing truths, one by one.

In hidden depths, our souls entwine,
A dance of currents, so divine.
Flowing gently, like a sigh,
The heart once hidden learns to fly.

Limbs of Time in the Abyss

In the abyss where shadows creep,
Limbs of time weave dreams they keep.
Every second, a fleeting ghost,
Echoing memories we cherish most.

Branches stretch, entwined and vast,
Holding moments, shadows cast.
Time's embrace can twist and turn,
In the depths, our hearts will yearn.

Silent whispers brush the past,
Reminders of shadows that never last.
We reach for echoes, out of sight,
Longing to grasp the fading light.

Yet in the dark, a spark remains,
The pulse of time through joys and pains.
In the abyss, we find our way,
With limbs of time, night turns to day.

As ages shift beneath our feet,
We stand resilient, strong, and fleet.
With every heartbeat, we transcend,
The limbs of time, our truest friend.

Unveiling the Quiet Depths

In the quiet depths where waters sigh,
Secrets linger, drift, and fly.
A silent world beneath the waves,
Embracing wonders, hidden caves.

Gifting visions in gentle sways,
Unveiling truths in myriad ways.
Every ripple holds a tale,
Whispered softly, as dreams set sail.

In dusky shades, reflections rise,
The heart unfolds, wise and wise.
In silence, we confront our fears,
As the ocean's heart holds our tears.

Beneath the surface, hope takes flight,
Guiding lost souls toward the light.
Each moment cherished, softly kept,
In the depths of quiet, the past has slept.

So linger here beneath the tide,
In these depths, let hope abide.
For in the stillness, peace we find,
The quiet depths, forever entwined.

Beneath the Glimmering Skin

Underneath the glowing hue,
Lies a heart encased in blue.
Waves of warmth, a fragile sheen,
Secrets lurk, yet remain unseen.

Beneath the stars, the whispers play,
Echoes of love that drift away.
Fleeting moments, soft and bright,
Cloaked in shadows, lost to night.

Veils of light hide every scar,
Softly shimmering from afar.
Each glimmer tells a quiet tale,
In the silence, dreams set sail.

The skin reflects the world so wide,
While the soul seeks refuge inside.
In the stillness, truths ignite,
Burning softly, shining bright.

Yet in the glow, we find our fears,
The weight of past, a cascade of tears.
But underneath, a strength resides,
A phoenix rising, love abides.

Submerged Thoughts and Dreamscapes

Beneath the surface, voices sigh,
Ripples of hope in the midnight sky.
Thoughts entwined, a delicate thread,
In the depths where shadows tread.

Silent currents, drift away,
Carrying dreams that crave the day.
Fragments flicker like distant stars,
Floating gently, healing scars.

In the deep, the mind takes flight,
Shimmering visions emerge from night.
Colors blend in a swirling dance,
Lost in a mesmerizing trance.

Bubbles rise, the surface breaks,
New horizons as the memory wakes.
In stillness lies the heart's embrace,
Breathing life into this sacred space.

Underwater, the world unfolds,
Secrets spoken, yet never told.
Submerged thoughts, like gentle streams,
Swim through the fabric of our dreams.

The Unraveled Tapestry

Threads of gold and shadows weave,
Stories hidden, waiting to cleave.
Each knot a laugh, each tear a sigh,
In tangled paths where memories lie.

Colors fading, yet still they glow,
Echoes of laughter in ebb and flow.
Patterns shift under time's caress,
Life's design, both joy and mess.

With every tug, the weave unwinds,
Revealing secrets, the heart finds.
Beneath the layers, soft and bright,
Lives a spark waiting for the light.

In the fray, a story spins,
Loss and love, the way it begins.
Tangled threads, a life's embrace,
In the chaos, we find our place.

But as we weave, know this truth,
The tapestry holds the spirit of youth.
Every stitch, a moment we sew,
In the fabric of life, we continue to grow.

Shadows Lurking in Still Water

Reflections cast upon the glass,
Silhouettes where moments pass.
Quiet ripples of the night,
Shadows dance just out of sight.

In the stillness, whispers creep,
Darkened secrets, silence deep.
Beneath the calm, a stirring dread,
Ghosts of dreams that went unsaid.

Waves of memory surge and fall,
Echoing wishes that once were tall.
Lingering doubts in soft twilight,
Flicker faintly, then take flight.

Beneath the surface, a world untold,
Tales of yearning, shadows bold.
As the moonlight gently fades,
Ghostly figures become parades.

Yet in these depths, a truth unfolds,
Life's still water, brave and cold.
In shadows, there's beauty and grace,
A dance of light and dark we embrace.

Currents of Concealed Truths

Whispers float on gentle streams,
Secrets hidden, wrapped in dreams.
Beneath the surface, shadows play,
Echoes of what we can't display.

Tides of time erase the signs,
While longing hearts draw fragile lines.
In the depths, intentions lie,
Caught between the sea and sky.

A silent battle rages on,
In tangled depths where hope is drawn.
Every wave a story tells,
Of truth concealed in ocean swells.

With every ebb, the past retreats,
And with the flow, new life competes.
In currents dark, the unknown waits,
For those who dare to challenge fates.

The ocean holds both light and shade,
A vast expanse where dreams are made.
In silent depths, the truth shall swim,
Among the waves, both strong and dim.

The Heart of the Ocean

In the deep, where silence reigns,
The heart of the ocean softly gains.
Each pulse a rhythm, strong yet calm,
Embracing sailors with its balm.

Whirls of blue and shades of green,
A canvas painted, rarely seen.
In hidden realms where wonders bloom,
The ocean's heart dispels all gloom.

Every tide a tale untold,
Of treasures lost and legends bold.
In shimmering depths, mysteries spark,
A dance of light within the dark.

The siren's song calls out to me,
A sweet allure from the endless sea.
I follow where the currents lead,
To find what lies beneath the greed.

So take my hand, we'll drift away,
Through waves of night and hues of day.
Together in the ocean's heart,
As timeless souls, we won't depart.

Underneath the Calm

Underneath the calm facade,
Rests a world that feels so odd.
Ripples dance, concealing strife,
In the quiet, hides the life.

Secrets murmur in the foam,
Tides that bring both loss and home.
In tranquil waves, a storm may brew,
A game of fate, unmasking true.

Beneath the surface, shadows glide,
Whispers echo, hearts collide.
For every peace, a tempest near,
In stillness, often lurks our fear.

Yet in the depths, resilience grows,
Where strength arises, beauty flows.
We navigate the calm and storm,
For heartfelt truths can break the norm.

Together, let us ride the waves,
Embrace the deep, where passion saves.
In every ebb, a chance to see,
The vibrant life that flows in me.

Tides of the Unexplored

Tides of the unexplored invite,
To venture forth into the night.
In every swell, a new surprise,
A realm of wonder 'neath the skies.

Footprints washed away by time,
Echoes whispering in the grime.
What lies beyond the horizon's edge,
A dance of fate on nature's ledge.

Discoveries in every wave,
In unseen worlds, our spirits crave.
The thrill of journeys yet to start,
Adventures pulsing in the heart.

With every tide, we chase the unknown,
In depths of blue, where seeds are sown.
The ocean calls, our spirits soar,
To find what waits on distant shores.

So let us sail the waters wide,
Embracing all that lies inside.
For in the depths, we find our way,
Through tides of life, come what may.

The Silent Call of the Deep

Beneath the waves, a whispered song,
Where shadows dance, and secrets belong.
The ocean's breath, a gentle sigh,
Calls to the brave, those willing to try.

In depths where light begins to fade,
Ancient tales of time are laid.
Creatures roam in midnight's cloak,
In silence, dreams and thoughts provoke.

A journey through the azure maze,
Each ripple hides a world ablaze.
The depths invite with whispered lore,
Echoes of life forevermore.

Tranquil tides that hide and seek,
Hold stories vast, a voice unique.
Beneath the surface, mysteries dwell,
In silence, depths have much to tell.

Dive deep, embrace the tranquil call,
For in the dark, we find our all.
The silent rhythm, a heartbeats' keep,
Awakens souls from slumber deep.

Exploring the Heart of Darkness

In shadows thick, where lost truths lie,
A flicker of hope, a fleeting sigh.
The path is rough, but courage found,
In twisted roots, and haunted ground.

The forest breathes a mystic air,
Within its grasp, the brave will dare.
Whispered fears in the branches sway,
Guide the heart as night turns to day.

Through tangled thorns and echoes loud,
The mind's own beast, a daunting shroud.
Yet every turn unveils a spark,
To illuminate the world's dark arc.

Among the gloom, the stars ignite,
Beneath the cloak, a flickering light.
We journey forth, with dreams in tow,
Embracing darkness, to truly know.

In silence deep, the truth shall gleam,
Stripped of illusion, we find our dream.
Exploring depths that threaten to bind,
Unlocking treasures within the mind.

The Subtle Art of Discovery

In quiet moments, secrets lie,
Soft whispers float on winds that sigh.
A glance, a touch, the world awakes,
In every heartbeat, new breath takes.

The painter's stroke, the sculptor's line,
Unveils the beauty, design divine.
Each journey starts with gentle leaps,
Through tranquil waters, the spirit keeps.

A flower blooms, despite the frost,
In every loss, find what's not lost.
The subtle art speaks loud and clear,
To open hearts, to quell all fear.

From hidden paths to skies of blue,
Every step teaches something new.
In exploration, wonder swells,
Moments captured, life's stories tell.

In tiny spaces, vastness grows,
With every breath, a new hope glows.
The subtle dance of fate unfolds,
In whispered truths, the world beholds.

Tides of Concealed Wonders

The moonlight pulls the ocean's face,
Where secrets sleep in gentle embrace.
Beneath the tides, the world is cast,
In liquid dreams, both slow and fast.

Waves that crash against the shore,
Unearth the tales of folklore lore.
With every ebb, a newness calls,
In every flow, the past enthralls.

Octopuses dance in seaweed's arms,
Coral gardens, with vibrant charms.
Each current hides a whispered tale,
Of journeys ventured, paths we sail.

The tides conceal what we must seek,
In murky depths, the brave will speak.
To find the gems where shadows lie,
Transforms the heart, and lifts it high.

As stars align with ocean's glow,
We journey forth, through high and low.
The hidden wonders always share,
In nature's heart, the secrets bare.

Secrets Beneath the Sand

Whispers held by grains of time,
Lost stories wrapped in quiet rhyme.
The sun-kissed dunes keep secrets tight,
Beneath the surface, hidden light.

Buried dreams in golden waves,
Echo history, the lost and brave.
Footprints fade, yet tales remain,
In every breath, the whispered pain.

Ancient treasures beneath the guise,
Silent truths and longing sighs.
A world unseen, yet deeply felt,
Where hearts in silence gently melt.

The shifting sands a timeless dance,
Holding memories in every glance.
Nature's breath, a soft caress,
In every grain, a hidden quest.

Secrets rise with every tide,
The wind, a friend, that will not hide.
With every storm, the past will sing,
Of all the wonders time will bring.

Beneath the Shimmering Surface

Reflections dance on waters bright,
Beneath the calm, a world ignites.
Shadows stir where secrets dwell,
In silent depths, they weave their spell.

Crystals glint in sunlight's touch,
A realm that holds so very much.
Each ripple tells a whispered tale,
Of love and longing, soft and frail.

Life teems in vibrant, hidden hues,
A tapestry of joyful blues.
Underneath, the currents sway,
Chasing dreams that drift away.

Bright fish swimming, darting fast,
In waters deep, they've found their past.
The surface shines, but what's below?
A world alive with ebb and flow.

Beneath the shimmer, stories flow,
Of hearts entwined and struggles slow.
Each wave that breaks, a sigh, a chance,
To dive beneath the deep expanse.

Waves of Solitude

In the hush of the ocean's roar,
A solitary heart, forever sore.
Each wave that crashes brings a thought,
Of battles lost and battles fought.

Moonlit tides in silent song,
Where echoes linger, deep and long.
Whispers of love on salted air,
Yet solitude is always there.

The sea stretches, vast and wild,
In its embrace, a lonely child.
Footprints washed away by time,
A symphony of endless rhyme.

Yet in the depths, a flicker glows,
Memories rise where the seaweed grows.
In every swell, a sigh, a pain,
A heart finds peace amidst the rain.

Waves crash down, but still I stand,
In solitude, I understand.
For every storm that sweeps the shore,
Holds a promise of something more.

The Uncharted Depths

Into the blue where few have tread,
Lies untold wonders, dreams unsaid.
In the darkness, secrets bloom,
A realm alive, beyond the gloom.

Ancient whispers, mysteries breathe,
Where shadows weave and visions seethe.
Creatures gliding, gracefully bold,
Guardians of treasures untold.

Coral castles in hues so bright,
Dance with currents in silent flight.
Beneath the waves, a world unknown,
In silence, seeds of hope are sown.

Endless journeys in waters deep,
Calls to wanderers, echoes creep.
With every dive, the heart expands,
To seek the truth beneath the sands.

In uncharted depths, I lose my fears,
Embrace the waves, drown out the years.
The ocean's heart will cradle me,
As I explore what's meant to be.

Dreams in Dark Waters

In the stillness of the night,
Whispers call from below,
Dancing shadows in the light,
Where silent currents flow.

Beneath the surface, dreams take flight,
Glimmers of a hidden past,
Reflections flicker, soft and bright,
Moments fleeting, never last.

A dive into the depths we seek,
To find what lies beneath,
Secrets buried, soft yet bleak,
Carried by the ocean's breath.

Rippling echoes, dreams entwined,
In the dark waters' embrace,
With every wave, a story signed,
In the realm of time and space.

We navigate through thoughts uncharted,
Guided by the stars above,
In the realm where dreams have started,
Here we learn what it means to love.

The Hidden Spectrum

Beyond the veil of night and day,
Colors dance in quiet grace,
Invisible to those who stray,
In search of a brighter place.

In shadows, light of prismatic hue,
Whispers of the unseen truth,
A canvas painted just for few,
Where lies the spark of youth.

Every shade a tale of being,
Silent stories yet untold,
In the chaos, there's a freeing,
A spectrum hidden, brave and bold.

Glimpses caught in fleeting glances,
Moments bright yet often missed,
In the dance of fleeting chances,
Lies a beauty cloaked in mist.

Unlock the colors of your heart,
Let them shine with all their might,
In every hue, find your part,
In the spectrum of the night.

A Tapestry of Secrets

Threads of stories interweave,
In patterns rich and deep,
Each whisper shares what we believe,
In the secrets that we keep.

Stitched with laughter, torn with sorrow,
Each tale a tapestry spun,
Visions of a distant morrow,
Where shadows dance and hopes run.

Woven by hands both young and old,
A fabric stretched across the years,
In every knot, a truth unfolds,
In laughter, pain, and hidden fears.

Colorful threads blend and embrace,
Creating beauty from despair,
In this craft where dreams find place,
We weave our lives with tender care.

A tapestry, both frail and strong,
In every thread, a legacy,
Together we will find where we belong,
In this intricate mystery.

Unraveled by Time

The sands of time slip through our hands,
Each grain a whispered tale,
In the desert of our plans,
Where dreams sometimes grow pale.

Yet in the passing, wisdom sown,
A garden rich with years,
In every moment, seeds are grown,
Watered by our tears.

Memories swirl like autumn leaves,
Dancing on the winds of change,
Fragile beauty, heart believes,
In the chaos, we find strange.

Time's embrace both gentle, cruel,
Shapes our journey, paints our scars,
In every lesson, we learn the rule,
Of reaching for the distant stars.

So let the moments unravel slow,
In life's intricate design,
Embrace the ebb, the flow,
For tomorrow is a gift, divine.

Milton Keynes UK
Ingram Content Group UK Ltd.
UKHW021954151124
451186UK00007B/239